Pain Play For Everyone

Third Edition

Luna Carruthers
SubmissiveGuide.com

Pain Play For Everyone

Third Edition

Thank you for your support!
Luna Carruthers

Luna Carruthers
SubmissiveGuide.com

PAIN PLAY FOR EVERYONE

Copyright © 2020 by Luna Carruthers ALL RIGHTS RESERVED.

No part of this publication may be reproduced, distributed, or transmitted in any form or by any means, including photocopying, recording, or other electronic or mechanical methods, without prior written permission of the publisher, except in the case of brief quotations embodied in critical reviews and certain other noncommercial uses permitted by copyright law.

SubmissiveGuide.com

Preface

When I first wrote this book, it was just a little ebook on Submissive Guide called "Processing Pain." That was back in 2012. Since then I've been able to develop further techniques, gather information and knowledge from others, and feel that this edition is a more in-depth guide that will help even the more timid bottoms.

Pain does not have to be a bad thing and playing with a sadist Top is far more rewarding when we can do our part to make reactions and responses to pain, as well as how we process it, come out more naturally. Doing this is sure to bring you more fulfillment in play, get you further, break down walls and help you explore more of what pain play can do for your SM experiences.

This book is written for bottoms who engage in all varieties of play that involve experiencing pain, no matter why you do so. If you're a sadist Top, you can learn from this book as well! Helping your bottom work though pain, adopting more positive techniques and breaking down old negative habits can be a deeply meaningful way to play.

You'll learn how you experience pain, methods you adopt to deal with pain that benefit you positively or negatively, how to build a processing technique to use for playtime and relearn methods that will help you go further, experience more intense play and break through previous limits.

Pain Play For Everyone

Third Edition

Table of Contents

Preface...7
Introduction: A Personal Story of Being a Masochist...............13
1: The Many Benefits of Pain..17
    Why You Submit To Pain in Play.......................................19
2: The Feel-Good Hormone Cocktail......................................28
    Adrenaline..29
    Endorphins...31
    Oxytocin...33
    What is Sub Drop?..34
    My Best Piece of Advice for Sub Drop Recovery................37
3: Natural Pain Processes...40
    The Brain's Job in Pain Processing....................................46
    The Natural Pain Processing Methods...............................48
    Allow Yourself to Feel Pain...53
4: Negative Pain Management Techniques.............................57
5: The Pain Processing Secret Formula...................................64
    The Magic Combination...67
    Learning A Processing Technique.....................................68
    Rainbows and Fireworks...75
6: What Can Block Pain Management?...................................79
    The Invisible Barrier of Your False Edge............................86

7: Important Tips for Negotiating Pain Play......................................89
   Be More Specific About Pain – When a Tool is More Than Sting or Thud..90
   Types of Pain You Could See During a BDSM Scene:..................94
In Closing...102

Introduction: A Personal Story of Being a Masochist

I love consensual pain. I've never really thought about it or analyzed what that means really, but reading other people's blogs, articles, and forum posts has always helped me see that saying I'm masochist is just another huge personal term in BDSM as a whole. So, to think it through, this is what being a masochist means to me.

I eroticize pain. I get the most thrill from impact play; be it flogging, spanking, paddles, punching, slapping, kicking, canes or crops. Just thinking about these activities can stir my sexual responses. I like sting more than thud (more on the ambiguity of these two terms later) which I'm beginning to think is a rare thing. So many people I talk to cringe when I say I like sting. I've always interpreted thud to be kinda uneventful. Now don't get me wrong, I love the feel of a heavy flogger thudding across my back, but the masochist in me wants sting and feeds off of it. I get the most gratification from a mixture of sting and thud. I like intense and steady once I've made it to that happy place.

Constant pain like clothespins and nipple clamps or the swelling of areas while the blood flow is cut off is another delicious pain, but it's one that I have a tendency to struggle against. In this I know that I like the struggle, I like the feeling that I can't take one more minute and yet proving myself wrong over and over again. I like to tremble as the endorphins take hold and I like the buzzy feeling I get when the pain has reached the threshold. Going past the threshold is just pain, not pleasure at all. With constant pain, pushing me over the edge will max me out.

How I process the pain really depends on how I've gone into the scene. The easiest for me is to moan and groan and sigh, allowing my body to express itself any way I can. I tend to wiggle or struggle with and then against the pain. To relax a bit I have to get past this point. I have to progress to silence and acceptance. When the pain of the impact toy blurs with pleasure and is more muted no matter how fierce it may be is when I can find a zone that I love to sit in and probably could for hours. It is cathartic and feels healing in a way.

Another way I like to process pain is to bring out the tears. It's a release to cry and sob and let the natural expression of pain come out. It starts out small and can lead to screams and loud cries. In this state I think I could get the most personal satisfaction from. I feel that I can push myself past the tears then I've made it to some level beyond what I thought I could have pushed myself.

It's only been recently that Master has accepted that making me cry is okay. It used to be a full stop for him. Needless to say I crashed hard if he stopped then. I was just getting into it and then he'd stop because he thought my reaction was negative rather than positive. Many conversations later I think he's accepting that I will call red if I'm done.

One of the most embarrassing ways I communicate pleasure in pain is by laughing. I get this way on more occasions than I can count. He could be going at me with the paddle and it will be so painful that I laugh and laugh. I try to stop only to explode in laughter more. I don't know if it was harder for Master to accept this than the crying, but I know that I still have problems when I laugh. It just feels… out of place. I'm not mocking the scene at all, I swear. It just feels so darned painful that I have to let it out somehow.

So, being a masochist is my own personal definition of pain translation. I don't have an ache for pain very often but when I do I'm pretty good at telling Master I need something. We're open that way. Since Master has grown in his role we've been better at giving each other what we need at the right time.

As with everything I write, please take this information as one person's view on the topic. Your opinion may vary, and I'm thrilled that it might be. Even if that is the case, I imagine there is something from this book that you can add to your own submissive journey. These are only my ideas and experiences, and your personal training and skill sets may be different. Feel free to customize any of the suggestions to fit your needs.

Let's get started.

1: The Many Benefits of Pain

If you don't identify as a masochist asking why you participate in pain play can be a question with no clear answer. Some say, "it is part of submission,", others "to please their Sadistic Top," and still others can say, "the benefits are endorphins and adrenaline rushes." No matter your reasoning for why you submit to pain play, being able to expand your ability to process pain and move through pain in a healthy and productive way is a great benefit to our role. Each of our D/s relationships is unique and as submissives we can choose to experience pain from our

1: The Many Benefits of Pain

Dominant's hand or we don't. There's room for all sorts of variations in the spectrum.

Why You Submit To Pain in Play

For those of us who participate in pain play, it is important to understand what we get from experiencing pain in a play aspect. These are just a few of the benefits of experiencing pain in play.

What is the benefit of pain for you? What are you seeking when you play?

I'm Seeking An Act Of Service

For submissives who may not identify as masochists but participate in pain play for the pleasure of their Tops, the goal of pain processing can be service. In this method it's not a matter of enduring the play but also giving of themselves so that their Top will be pleased. Learning positive pain processes will help that moment of service last longer and be more rewarding. Even if you do identify as masochistic in some form, an act of service could be trying something you have on your limits list in the "maybe" column, or pushing your boundaries a bit to see just where the edge is for you.

The methods of processing pain you're about to learn in this book, can help you to endure pain longer, go further and continue to be obedient without breaking down or using your safeword. All because you learned a few simple techniques and broke down any negative pain processing you may have learned up to now.

I'm Seeking Sub Space

The ultimate goal for many submissives in pain play is that elusive 'space' called sub space. To reach it is to be in utter peace and bliss. Sub space is the trance-like, out-of-body-like, floaty good feelings that submissives can get lost in during play or service.

The endorphins that are released during pain play can lead to a feeling of light-headedness, euphoria and sometimes out of body-like experiences. In most people this happens due to intense pain processing and sensations related to it. Working to learn pain processing techniques can help you develop an understanding for how your body reacts to the endorphins and if you can release and let yourself float into sub space or not.

Some of the more common symptoms of sub space include:
- Lightheaded
- Disassociated from reality
- Inability to speak
- Slow reactions to sensation, including pain
- Difficulty in comprehending speech or direction
- Intense pleasure
- Out of body sensations
- Hyperactivity
- Child-like behavior
- Giggling
- Loss of Time
- Sense of peace or tranquility

1: The Many Benefits of Pain

Not everyone who enjoys pain play gets to sub space – it is related completely on your body's ability to process pain and how you respond to your body. You aren't a good or bad person if you can't get to sub space and I highly recommend not making it the goal of every single play session. If you are partnered with a sadist Top, they are not going to want their partner in sub space every time they play. Why? The responses that sadists feed off of, your reactions to pain, completely stop when you reach this altered state, making the enjoyment that they would get out of giving pain disappear.

That's not to say that some Tops don't enjoy getting their bottoms to sub space. It can be a very freeing feeling to know that you are in such a relaxed and trusting place to allow the Top to care for you during sub space.

I'm Seeking Catharsis

For some submissives, pain play as a way to escape or to allow our emotions free reign. There are numerous times I have asked for a healing flogging from my partner because I needed to release stress or have some sadness or anger to process. It's not a substitute for professional therapy, but in a pinch it can really do a lot for a submissive's mood. Administered pain can be an excellent tool for stress relief and catharsis. Pain given in this way is usually steady and rhythmic. It has a constant pain level so that the bottom won't get jolted with pain, but endure a regular repetitive dose. A thuddy flogger or a heavy paddle is likely to work better than a session with a crop or whip because of the constant drumming sensation that thuddy tools bring to the scene.

Often, a healing pain session ends with crying or screaming or intense emotional outpouring of other sorts. It can even help you slip into sub space, if that's your goal. The Top is like a therapist that knows just what level of pain you need to get you to express your bottled up emotions, or uses the pain to get you to let go of responsibility. It requires a huge level of trust and connection for this to work.

1: The Many Benefits of Pain

I'm Seeking Pleasure

For some bottoms, pain is a direct link to pleasure. It is often said that the line between pain and pleasure is blurred and for these bottoms that line is easily crossed. Pain for this person brings sexually heightened emotions, pleasure and often, orgasms. For others still, pain **IS** the pleasure. The sensations of pain, usually intense pain is what turns them on and drives them to an intimacy that isn't shared with anyone other than the Top administering to them.

Mixing pain and pleasure is a common relation in SM play, and worth thinking about. Pain and pleasure are very close to each other on the sensation spectrum and for many people they can and do overlap.

Blurring the Lines of Pain and Pleasure

I'm going to paint you a picture. Before I do so I'm going to make a few assumptions about you and your sexual background. First, I assume that you are sexually active and

Processing Pain

have, or have had, a steady partner. Second, I assume that you have been active long enough that you have experienced many of the different lovemaking positions available to you.

I am going to assume that while having sex with your partner, at one time or other, you have been on top with your partner laying on his back. While on top, your partner has had full access to your breasts and has taken full advantage of that position.

Let's assume that at some point in time you have leaned forward just a little bit so that your lover could take your nipples into their mouth. They nibble them and you both are getting closer to orgasm. The closer you get, the more excited they become and the more aggressively they nibble. You feel little twinges of pain mixed with the good feeling of their nibbles. Not enough pain to kill your erotic feeling but enough to add that extra bit of stimulation that brings you closer to climax. They are getting closer, you are getting closer, the nibbling intensifies and in moments you find yourself...

STOP!!!!!!

1: The Many Benefits of Pain

Just before you reach that magic moment, I want for you to stop and remove yourself from that situation. Place yourself, if you will, walking in your local shopping mall. If someone were to walk up to you at that very minute and squeeze your nipple with the exact amount of pressure that you were receiving with your lover, you would scream out in pain without a doubt. However, back in bed, you were about to scream out for a much different and much more enjoyable reason.

So the idea that some painful situations actually feel good is not as strange as you might think. Consider Also, those feel good chemicals we talked about have a lot to do with reducing the brain's response to pain and can in fact make it less painful and more pleasant to help us cope with increasing stress of the situation.

Why Does It Matter What I'm Seeking?

When you only service someone else's needs, and neglect to see any personal value in receiving pain play it makes it harder for you to relax and focus on processing. Service is great, I'm a service submissive myself, but I still find more confidence in what I do if I find a reason for me to do whatever it is I'm doing.

There are methods in this book that will help you relax and explore what your body is telling you, so that even if you aren't a masochist and you are submitting to pain for your Dominant's pleasure, you can help yourself get what you might need from it. Even if that's reassurance that you can serve your Dominant in a way you thought you couldn't.

2: The Feel-Good Hormone Cocktail

Before we get into discussing what pain processing is and how to maximize the benefits, we need to understand how our body responds to pain play. The two key chemical components to enjoying pain play are adrenaline and endorphins. A supporting chemical that happens in some situations is oxytocin. These chemicals are released into the bloodstream shortly after you begin an intense situation and stay high for as long as the body needs them to manage the emotional and physical stress we put our bodies though.

Adrenaline

Also known as epinephrine, when secreted into the bloodstream, it rapidly prepares the body for action in emergency situations. We call this the "fight or flight" response.

The hormone boosts the supply of oxygen and glucose to the brain and muscles, while suppressing other non-emergency bodily processes (digestion in particular).

It increases heart rate and stroke volume, dilates the pupils, and constricts blood vessels in the skin and gastrointestinal tract while dilating them in skeletal muscles. It elevates the blood sugar level also.

Most sadomasochistic play will only trigger low levels of adrenaline. If you've ever felt the butterflies in your stomach, anxiety or the desire to run and hide to escape then you've probably felt a bit of adrenaline flowing and you are reacting to it. The blood rush and excited feelings can be

2: The Feel-Good Hormone Cocktail

addictive, which is where the term adrenaline junkies come from.

Endorphins

Stress and pain are the two most common factors for the release of endorphins. Endorphins then interact with receptors in the brain to reduce our perception of pain and act similarly to drugs such as morphine and codeine. The increasing dose of endorphins during play reduces the pain further and those morphine-like high notes get stronger.

Endorphins released in the brain react with the part of brain cells called opioid receptors. It's the same part of nerve cells that are affected by drugs like morphine, codeine and the like. However, while outside opiates like morphine are highly addictive, endorphins are not considered to be so. You might think that's because natural chemicals in the body can't be as strong as pharmaceutical ones, but you would be wrong. Of the 20 or so kinds of endorphin chemicals in the brain at least one of them (called beta-endorphins) are stronger than morphine.

2: The Feel-Good Hormone Cocktail

Endorphins have the happy effect of blocking pain as well as giving you a sense of euphoria. They also cause you to have a higher pain tolerance once they kick in and lower your emotional inhibitions. It's the stuff that causes "runner's high" in long distance runners, but I think getting spanked is a much more fun way to get there. The two major triggers for your body's natural drug are pain and stress. During a scene, typically both of those things are in abundant supply. So what does that mean for masochistic bottoms? It means that we can get high during play.

Oxytocin

Oxytocin is a hormone secreted by the pituitary gland. It is sometimes called the "cuddle hormone" or the "love hormone" because it is released when people snuggle or bond socially. It can also intensify memories of bonding gone bad, such as in bad breakups or abusive relationships with parents. How oxytocin makes you feel depends on the environment. It is often released during sexual activity and linked to the intensity of orgasms.

The whole hormone cocktail does a number on your body and mind, causing sub space in some people and once the hormones leave your bloodstream you face withdrawal. That's called sub drop.

You do not have to experience sub space to go through sub drop.

2: The Feel-Good Hormone Cocktail

What is Sub Drop?

When you play and it gets really intense, you feel great. You don't want it to end and that happy, buzzy feeling carries on for a while after play. We all love that feeling, but what happens when that feeling starts to go away? What if instead of good or even normal you feel ill, sad, depressed and troubled? You've encountered sub drop.

Sub drop can come in many different forms. Sub drop is the body's response to the drop of the hormone cocktail in the body after a play session. Most of what you read online are the physical aspects; the fatigue, sadness, aches and pains and recovery from marks.

The real range of symptoms is vast and personal. While most of it is physical in nature, there are emotional side effects as well. We'll try to cover the physical as well as the emotional struggle we can put ourselves through recovering from play.

Physical Symptoms

- Fatigue
- Crying
- Aches and pains
- Stomach aches
- Cold hands and/or feet
- Stiffness
- Cravings for sweets
- Chills
- Headaches
- Nausea
- General malaise

Emotional Symptoms

- Sadness or melancholy
- Anxiety/Agitation
- Depression
- Fear
- Confusion

2: The Feel-Good Hormone Cocktail

- Guilt
- Shame

There is a more intense side of sub drop that gets very little attention because for each person it is different and describing how to recover can take many forms.

If not cared for, you could go into depression just from one play session. The endorphins and other hormones like adrenaline and oxytocin, released during play leave your body in such a way that it takes the time to rebuild the balance of hormones in your system. You could feel like you have a hangover or partied too hard the night before, you could feel lost and depressed for hours or days. You may just want to sleep it off. These are the more extreme forms of drop. Some people recover in a matter of hours, but others could exhibit signs of sub drop for weeks after an intense session.

My Best Piece of Advice for Sub Drop Recovery

Sub drop is hard. The many times that it's hit me the hardest have been the biggest opportunity for me to learn about my reactions, my feelings and what I'm thinking. The best piece of advice I can give you is that should embrace the experience and prepare for the next time. I know we are sad, stressed, lonely, depressed and a variety of other low impact emotions when in sub drop, but once you are aware of what's going on you can learn from it and how to make the next drop less severe.

You can learn to lessen the effects that sub drop has on your body and mind. If you feel sad, find things to do that make you happy. Are you experiencing physical exhaustion or a sense of illness? Get rest, take your vitamins and take care of yourself. Are you lonely? Then make a date with friends to catch up. You can feel better, you just have to make it happen and doing a bit of preparation will go a long way to making that happen.

2: The Feel-Good Hormone Cocktail

Sub drop doesn't have to have such a huge impact on your after playtime moments. With a bit of preparation and awareness, you can not only reduce some of it but use it to help you communicate with your partners and express yourself.

Don't be ashamed that you dropped. No matter how much experience you have, you may drop. Even if you haven't had sub drop in years, a particularly intense scene could leave you droopy. It's okay. Just take care of yourself.

A Drop Kit

Lastly, it might help you to have all your needs for sub drop together in a central location. You can put it together before you play or have a dedicated bag for sub drop recovery. What would you put in it? Well, that depends on what you need to feel better after play. Blankets, teddies, and Gatorade are common. Pain meds, your journal, fun movies, bubble bath or shower bombs, restaurant gift cards, sentimental bits and bobs and more.

A drop kit can be helpful for Dominants and submissives that experience moderate to severe drop after play sessions. The drop can be associated with feelings of loneliness, mental and physical exhaustion, confusion, insecurity, tremors, and many other physical symptoms. It is important to take care of yourself during times of drop. This kit will put all the things necessary at your fingertips.

I know that while you are experiencing sub drop that it can be overwhelming and scary but with the right tools and knowledge at your disposal you can help lessen and prevent some of the really strong side effects. Prepare for the potential of sub drop, even if you don't think you'll experience it.

3: Natural Pain Processes

Sadomasochism, the term that combines sadism and masochism, is the giving and receiving of sensations. In a lot of cases this also includes pain. Many of the sadomasochistic tendencies bleed into our relationships in some form or other so what better discussion than to talk about processing pain. Over the next few pages we'll cover what the natural pain process is, pain management techniques, how to learn a management technique to help you better in play and overcoming the false edge that keeps us from reaching our true potential.

Everyone you meet has different methods for how they handle pain. You could describe them as the "hold it ins," the "pain dancers," the "cursing crowd" and even the "criers." You have even more methods in between. How you handle pain is a result of nature and nurture. Perhaps as you were a child you heard the phrase, "walk it off," or "let me kiss it and make it feel better." These are ways we've learned to handle pain.

When you engage in playtime with a Dominant your body is the canvas for sensation and pleasure. You can run the gamut of emotions and many of them can take you by surprise. It's not uncommon even for someone who plays regularly to be shocked by a new reaction to a play activity that they have experienced before. This goes beyond the welts, bruises, scratches and other physical marks from play. Let's cover a few of the more common reactions to play.

Shivers

Shivers are brought on by adrenaline in your system. It's a natural coping mechanism when dealing with pain and is why a lot of people who go into shock from trauma start shivering. Not all people will shiver because of adrenaline though. Some shiver because of nervousness. During nervous shivers, your inactive mind sends a message to all your body parts without telling your active mind to control the normal functioning of your body. This will cause the slight trembles.

Dizziness/Light-headed

When you feel dizzy or light-headed this could signal an episode of low blood sugar. You do not have to be diabetic to get low blood sugar. Everyone reacts differently to fluctuations in their blood glucose levels. Some symptoms of non-diabetic hypoglycemia may include:

- dizziness
- a feeling of extreme hunger
- a headache
- confusion
- an inability to concentrate
- sweating
- shaking
- blurred vision
- personality changes

It can happen when you haven't had enough to eat or drink before a session. I encourage you to eat right and get enough to drink at least 30 minutes before playing. You can keep sports drinks on hand during play to make sure you are well hydrated. No one should continue playing when suddenly feeling ill, it is a sign of distress.

To aid someone suffering from a bout of low blood sugar makes sure you keep high carbohydrate simple sugars on hand; orange juice is a good suggestion. If not treated, the person could go into shock or become unconscious.

Crying

Tears are a normal release of emotions. They could be from the pain you are enduring or from bottled up emotions that all of a sudden come to the surface during play. Crying often has absolutely nothing to do with the scene playing out. A lot of times I play for catharsis, or because I want/need to cry and a good spanking or flogging can do that for me. It's almost as good as therapy! (I don't condone this as a direct substitute for therapy.)

Laughing

When we laugh there is an actual chemical change in our bodies that helps to ease pain and release stress. When I say stress, it's not the negative stress, but the physical pain we may be engaged in or the emotional and physical tension of the scene. Laughing helps to positively release that stress and encourages the body to improve pain tolerances. In a study published in September 2011 in the journal

"Proceedings of the Royal Society B: Biological Sciences (https://doi.org/10.1098/rspb.2011.1373)," found that laughter can increase pain tolerances up to 10%.

I'm known to break out in giggle fits during and immediately after an intense scene as a result of the endorphins running through my bloodstream. Endorphins cause different reactions in people and laughing happens to be one of mine.

The Brain's Job in Pain Processing

Our perception of pain is shaped by our brain circuits that are constantly filtering information coming in from our sensory nerves. Our brain can turn the volume of the pain information up or down depending on the situation. Knowing this, you can train your brain to do what you wish it to with the pain information that you receive during a consensual play session.

The brain uses three different systems to process pain information.

1. The **somatosensory cortex** determines the pain's location, intensity and characteristics: stabbing, aching, burning, etc.
2. The **frontal cortex** is in charge of thinking and processing how to react.
3. The **limbic system** exists for the emotional aspect of pain – the part that makes us go, "Ow!" or "Oooh!"

The end result of a pin prick, for example, is that you feel a sensation of pain in your finger, think "Ouch! What was that?" or something similar, and react emotionally to the pain; e.g. you feel annoyed, irritated or cry.

Positive emotions like trust, feeling calm, and safe and connected can minimize pain. Negative emotions tend to have the opposite effect. Torturers have exploited that aspect for centuries.

With that in mind you may begin to see how a well thought out SM scene might employ elements of building negative emotions to make a bottom's reactions to pain more genuine. Or how building trust and confidence in a top could push you further than you thought possible before.

The Natural Pain Processing Methods

There are three relatively natural pain processing methods we are going to talk about first. They are acceptance, denial and devouring. Two of these methods are very common, and the third while being rare happens to be where masochism meets euphoria.

Acceptance

The acceptance method of pain management is the original method that we are born with. In this method we experience pain fully. We don't try to escape the pain or dull the pain but allow it to wash over us. As a child the only thing we know to do is hurt when something hurts. It's only as we grow up and learn to 'deal' with pain that we push it down into ourselves, try to ignore it and dissipate it with several methods that we'll be talking about through the course of this book.

Acceptance is also where most sub space occurs during play. When we stop fighting our reactions to the pain and really feel and experience the sensations we are receiving we can get in touch with the endorphins and adrenaline at play in our bodies. Later on we'll be talking about how to learn pain processing techniques to make your play more worthwhile and allow yourself to experience many levels of pain and sensation.

Rejection

In the rejection method, much as you might think, is where you refuse to accept pain. Because of this you only perceive a fraction of the pain.

Rejection is usually a result of being taught that showing pain is a sign of weakness. People who manage pain this way have trained themselves to deny the pain either consciously or subconsciously. It's likely that as a child this person was told to stop crying many times and that the pain wasn't as bad as they were making it out. Inside they learned to stuff the pain down and show no signs that something hurt. Adults that have had this processing method ingrained are ones you often see who hurt themselves and are silent, squeezing their eyes shut and they visibly hold the pain in.

Another way that rejection can play out is when someone constantly tells you, "it doesn't hurt that much," while limping. Society, in my opinion, has falsely determined that it's not manly to cry and it's not masculine to show fear or pain. That men are not supposed to experience pain in the same way women do. Hopefully we can teach our children that pain is something natural to experience and how you respond is natural to you.

As a masochist, rejection gets in the way of your ultimate goal which is the enjoyment of the pain. If you keep telling yourself that you can take it while tensing your muscles and clenching your teeth then you are likely rejecting the pain. If you've been trained to be motionless while receiving pain it's possible you've taught yourself a rejection technique (however some people use an acceptance process for this as well).

Devouring

This is the most rare pain method. Extreme masochists typically identify with this management process. You may be wondering then, if so many people identify as masochist, why is the third pain processing method so rare? Many people, including myself, are considered masochist, but once you read the third method you will really see how rare and unique some masochists are. I've never met a masochist such as this and I can't wait till I get the opportunity!

When someone devours the pain it becomes energy. The person doesn't experience pain as pain but more as raw energy or excitement. These people get a pure charge from the pain. Masochists with this processing method tend to look really happy, like they are on drugs while being inflicted with pain. Instead of a cathartic feeling, a person after play that has used the pain as energy will be bubbly, energetic and in good spirits. Aftercare for a devouring bottom is different than bottoms that use the other types of processing.

Devouring is not limited to those special masochists; you can learn devouring techniques as a part of your personal pain management. It is not an easy process and not one I can help you learn through a book. I have yet to get there myself!

Now, no matter what processing method you use, there are ways you can learn to process pain differently to enjoy pain play more fully, allow you to take more pain and to push your pain edge further.

Allow Yourself to Feel Pain

We've taught ourselves a multitude of ways to reject and ignore pain, so one of the first challenges for anyone learning to explore pain play is to allow yourself to feel pain.

For pain play to work we need to rewrite those sequences and allow ourselves to feel the full experience of pain, to allow it to wash over us, to overcome us and to overwhelm us. Through this, we can begin to learn to process pain in a beneficial way and Tops can benefit from our positive responses.

If you find yourself struggling and fighting the pain you have to start here before you can learn a processing technique. It is very likely that you will not be able to play for long and it will be hard, but once you can accept the full experience of pain you can then learn to control it and use it to you and your Top's benefit.

One way to do this is to learn a meditation technique. Once you are able to quiet your mind and allow the world to pass by without your interaction you can begin to see pain as more than something to fight against.

Learn a Simple Meditation

That's right. If you can quiet your mind you will be able to quiet your body. This is going to take more than a day to learn. I'd recommend trying it everyday until you can sit quietly for at least 15 minutes.

There are many books on how to meditate, but the one I recommend is The Miracle of Mindfulness: An Introduction to the Practice of Meditation by Thich Nhat Hanh (http://amzn.to/1xu8al1), a Vietnamese monk, a renowned Zen master, a poet, and a peace activist.

Try This!

Sit comfortably with your spine straight. You may choose to sit in a chair or on the floor cross-legged as long as you can maintain the position for at least 15 minutes. Do not lie down as this encourages drowsiness.

Now close your eyes and draw your attention to your breath. Notice how the breath enters your body through your nostrils and exits out of your mouth. Focus your attention on the places where your breath enters and exits. If thoughts or feelings surface – and they will – simply return your focus back to your breathing. Count your breaths. Start with ten and work your way up. Then slowly open your eyes and become aware of your surroundings.

As you learn to do this for longer periods you will be able to use these tactics when you need to. Your body will be able to take a mediation moment and your fight against pain should diminish.

I'm not saying this is easy; I don't have it down pat either. But I'm learning and progressing and that's the point. I'm better than I was a month ago and will continue to improve. I know you can too.

Next Steps

If bondage helps center you, try it during your meditation. It can help you focus on being silent and relaxing in your position.

Try to play some relaxing music while you hold your position. It's best to choose music without words so that your focus remains on your breath and not the words of the songs. Practice holding your positions for up to 15 minutes.

Final step is to try your meditation and quieting movements with a lot of distraction. If you can, try to do your mediation at a play party or munch. It need not be obvious, just relax your body and sit silently for awhile.

4: Negative Pain Management Techniques

If you ask any sadist what they enjoy out of pain play, it's likely going to be watching the bottom respond to the pain. The more response, the higher the enjoyment for the top. Why is this important? Well, if the method of pain management doesn't allow you to respond well to the pain, then the play will be less fulfilling for at least one, if not both of you. Ultimately we want to be able to have a wonderful responsive play time.

4: Negative Pain Management Techniques

Pain management is different from pain processing in that management techniques are how we learn to deal with pain; the natural processes are what are available to us at birth. You learn or pick up pain management techniques by example or through the way you were raised. Even being called a "cry baby" or being told to walk it off one too many times can retrain your brain on how to process the pain in a way that is detrimental to SM later in life.

Typically a person will employ many methods of pain processing in a single play session. Some combinations lead to sub space while others will lead to a heightened experience of sadism and masochism. Goals for everyone are unique and should be discussed as a part of negotiation before play begins.

The following three methods are the most negative in result.

Detachment

The first method of pain management I'm going to talk about is detachment. With detachment you separate your mind from your body so pain doesn't register in your mind. It's the most common pain management technique during sub space. A lot of descriptions of sub space are that the sub was above their body looking down and they could see what was happening but not feel it. This is detachment. As you can probably realize, most people don't start with this technique, but rather end up here.

Sub space is not negative for most people. It's a common goal for play since the bottom feels amazing and has become overwhelmed with the hormone cocktail. But they also lose all reactions, the ability to communicate in most cases and for pain processing, this is the exact opposite of what you are looking for.

Detachment is not what many masochists look for with pain play. Since the pain isn't experienced, the full pleasure of it is lost. Sadists also don't like their bottoms to detach from the pain because they don't get the responses and reaction from the pain they are looking for in a fulfilling scene. A purely SM scene will rarely end with subspace until a sadist is ready; a sadist will constantly bring the masochist away from the detachment phase to extend the play.

Compression

In compression, you try to internalize the pain and bury the pain deep inside. With each bit of pain you press it and stuff it down further until you can't feel it anymore. This method of pain management is most commonly associated with emotional pain, such as the denial phase of grief. It is also seen in pain play if this method is fresh on the person's mind or is a common stress avoidance technique. Common ways people visibly bury the pain is by clenching muscles such as jaws, hands and other large muscle masses. It's also easy to notice compression when someone holds their breath.

With compression, the bottom doesn't get most of the benefit of the pain experience and because of this the sadist also gets denied pleasure from feeding on the reactions of the bottom. What can be worse is that the unreleased, compressed pain turns into stress that will build over time until it is released. Compressed pain can cause headaches, fatigue and muscle cramps hours or days after play. If you compress pain, you could be causing your own sub drop.

Fight And Extinguish

The last negative method for pain management is force of will. In this method the person experiences pain by fighting it. The pain is snuffed out by the force of will; practically suffocating it. Someone using this method will still feel the pain more than through compression but you don't get the long term stress build up of compression. You do however

4: Negative Pain Management Techniques

feel immediate exhaustion and stress from the effort of fighting the pain. Someone who is fighting the pain is practically vibrating in their bondage, or sucks their breath in and out through pursed lips or clenched teeth and eyes squeezed shut in concentration. Fighters can also get angry and lash out at their partner during play.

As with the other negative ways to manage pain, you don't get the full benefits of the pain and neither does the sadist.

- Do you do any of these negative techniques?
- Why did I include detachment as a negative rather than a positive since subspace is so sought after?
- What do you think some positive techniques might be?

Unlearning a negative technique takes time, but the first step is awareness. If you can see yourself in any of the negative pain management techniques above, watch for them when you play and try to use the mediation techniques from earlier to embrace the sensations that are going on instead of fighting or rejecting them. In time, you may see a whole new side of pain sensations that leave you feeling better, not worse after a scene.

5: The Pain Processing Secret Formula

Now that we've learned the negative ways we manage pain during play I'd like to cover a couple of the ways that help us experience pain as something good for us and our partners. After all, if you engage in pain play you are wanting to experience the pain, right? As bottoms in a scene the benefit for experiencing pain is usually direct since we are the ones receiving pain. Don't forget though that part of your receiving is also an exchange for the top. They want to watch you process that pain in open and positive ways so that they can get energy from it.

Dispersion

My personal favorite way to manage pain is through dispersion. When you disperse pain it filters throughout the body, radiating away from the point of pain. It still hurts but is less intense. This method allows you to play longer and get more benefit from the pain by making it tolerable. Visualizing heat or colors is a common way to disperse pain.

It's also great for the sadist because the reactions are still there and responses from pain still cue them into the experience.

Coming up I will be talking about ways to disperse pain as well as releasing it. It's a great combo that every bottom should have in their arsenal if pain play is on the menu.

5: The Pain Processing Secret Formula

Release

Releasing pain is typically the final result of any pain you experience. At some point you are going to have to let the pain go from the body. Most people get the greatest benefit from releasing the pain. It works with emotional pain and stress as well. Release has a cleansing effect. Vocalizations and vigorous movements are all a part of releasing the pain.

What's good about releasing pain is it's also the best experience for sadists. They can best experience your pain and allows both of you to play longer and harder and get more out of play.

The Magic Combination

The best way to process pain is to **accept the pain, disperse it and then release it**. Acceptance is a natural process that we've had at birth. Then we use the two positive methods to help us enhance our pain management in the best possible way.

Putting it all together, you can experience the pain, make it less intense and you get the most benefit from the pain. You don't get the immediate or long term build up of stress that some negative pain management techniques can do. This combination works well to release emotional pain and stress that you may be experiencing. In a scene where you accept, disperse and release the pain a sadist gets the most benefit and the bottom is rewarded as well.

Get ready to learn a pain processing technique to make everything beneficial and encourage enhanced playtime!

5: The Pain Processing Secret Formula

Learning A Processing Technique

Pain processing is natural to a certain extent. For some people—boys more than girls—an additional degree of pain processing is taught from a very early age, but not always in the healthiest way. Boys learn they have to be tough, whereas girls are often taught to avoid situations that could be painful. Then there are the lucky few who, once they become involved in SM, intentionally continue their education in pain processing by noticing what works, and developing that; noticing what others do, and trying it; and by asking questions or taking classes to increase their pain-handling capabilities.

So how can you learn a pain processing technique?

Since pain management is personal it may be difficult to get people to talk about how they process pain, and they may not be really sure what they are doing in an SM scene. I recommend you take some time to watch the bottoms at a play party during a flogging or caning or other painful play. Keep your eye open for the pain management techniques that I've described previously.

Learning to accept pain has various methods. I suggest you practice these the next time you play and find one or more that work best for you. The best way to learn a processing technique is to practice.

5: The Pain Processing Secret Formula

Breathe

Women in labor who are asked to breathe through the pain aren't doing it just to distract themselves. It's been a long-known medical tactic that breathing rhythmically helps to lessen pain. According to researchers on a clinical trial at Arizona State University, halving the number of breaths per minute decreased pain. The average number of breaths per minute is 12 to 18, and slowing down to six had a significant effect. The researchers believed that "slowing breathing has a direct impact on the sympathetic nervous system, which helps control blood flow and skin temperature, blocking some of the pain response." (http://asunews.asu.edu/20100407_painstudy)

With this information you can deduce that holding your breath will not aid you in your pain processing, which is why it falls in the negative techniques we've talked about. A very easy way to start learning a pain processing method is to control your breathing, especially focusing on the breath immediately after an impact or initial pain. If you're able to time it, try to exhale at the onset of the pain for a count of 5.

Fantasy

Placing yourself into a fantasy role, or enacting a fantasy in your head while experiencing pain can act as a distraction to the pain; or, depending on the fantasy, work to enhance it. Pretending you are in a dream where the pain is expected can help your body tolerate the pain until it's ready to process and handle it in its own way. It's not uncommon to eventually drop the need for fantasy once your body can process pain in other more beneficial ways.

Visualization

The next three methods are the ways that I often use to process pain and for me, they work the best to reach and overcome the pain edge. They fall under visualizing pain.

1. **Light** – Seeing the pain come in as light and then dispersing it throughout your body is an excellent coping technique and is relatively easy to learn. Imagine the impact as a burst of light, from a pinprick and growing like a flash, spreading out across a larger surface on your body. For

5: The Pain Processing Secret Formula

example, if you receive a flogging strike and visualize it as light flashing across your back it will spread the pain; making it more tolerable.

2. **Heat** – Heat is a really easy visualization method also, because anyone on a receiving end of a spanking knows that your skin heats up as it is spanked. Taking that heat and using it to spread the pain, or to release it into the air as heat can be a way to accept more and greater forms of pain. In the same method as the light technique, use the heat to spread across your skin. That warmth can be soothing. It's also possible to take deep heat and visualize moving it to the surface, where it will be more tolerable.

3. **Color** – If you are good with visualizing light then adding color would be a good next step. This form of visualization can take on many forms, from seeing red or yellow or even white colors racing across the skin to imagining the colors shooting into the sky; taking the pain with it.

Storage

Novices to pain processing commonly have issues accepting pain as anything as pleasant as heat, color or light and so they may use an easily accessible pain technique called storage. In this case, the bottom accepts and stores the pain in the immediate vicinity of the site it is happening. Holding the pain in as long as possible, and then with warning to the Top, you release that pain in one action. You can release it by shaking, screaming, laughing, wiggling, cursing, or whatever works best for you.

Bottoms who wiggle and squeal throughout the entire scene and are encouraged to are using this technique but dispelling the stored energy almost immediately. In a larger play space or at parties this can be distracting and disturbing to other players. Constantly releasing the energy stroke by stroke is a lower pay off. You can't get the big pay off and this results in less intensity in responses and reduced fulfillment in play. Not to mention it is exhausting!

The next time you see a pain scene, understand that the bottom is likely working as hard as the top. Pain processing for the benefit of themselves and the Top is rewarding and exhausting work. It encourages good habits of breathing and centered presence, drawing you into the scene, opening you to its possibilities rather than letting you stew on its likely side effects. Scenes like this are magnetic and beautiful to see.

Rainbows and Fireworks

After a lot of practice processing pain I've found that I can move in and out of various types of positive pain processing in a single scene. I use one method for sharp, stingy sensations and another for deep thuddy ones. A favorite and most successful processing technique – which is actually two techniques combined, I call rainbows and fireworks.

Rainbows

The rainbow phase of pain processing is a visualization technique. If you are good at imagining color with a strike or blow then you could try this method – but don't let the focus move from away from the pain. There's no need to concentrate so hard on how to process pain that you miss the pain altogether, remember the point is to move fluidly through pain processing.

What happens during rainbows is that instead of a single color radiating from an impact, I imagine the start of a rainbow. The bold reds that fade to orange, yellow, and so on down to indigo and then gone. Sometimes the rainbow effect only gets to orange before another strike is delivered but if my partner is feeling generous I have enough time to process the blow and get all the way to blue and indigo before another rainbow starts. As the with the other color visualizations, the pain dissipates as the rainbow fades.

Fireworks

Fireworks is a storage technique. Remember that in a storage technique the bottom collects the pain and stores it until they can release it. This is a common occurrence for me during a caning. My Dominant likes to pile on a series of strikes, where the pain gets bigger and more intense, and then pause. In that pause I'm able to let go of the pain. He's working with my pain processing in that moment instead of against it.

At the stage of release I tend to swirl my hands around and wiggle my fingers wildly. If my hands are bound then the fireworks come out of my toes. You can visualize this as holding a sparkler and swirling it around or the small firework pinwheels that spin around when lit. I see the pain flying out of my fingertips in circles and arcs like those fireworks would. They burst forth pretty aggressively if the pain has piled up quite a bit.

I realize that my personal processing techniques might not work for you, I've been practicing them for quite some time. But I hope that you can see that everyone processes differently and with time you too can have something that works well for you in any pain play situation.

Practice the different methods described in this chapter and find ones that are easy for your to adopt. Start using them to see how far you can travel through pain and perhaps go just a bit further than you have in the past. Also, keep an eye on

5: The Pain Processing Secret Formula

how you feel in the hours and days afterward. Are you less exhausted, how was your sub drop symptoms? Good pain processing can, as we've discussed, reduce or eliminate some of your more exceptionally bad recovery time.

6: What Can Block Pain Management?

What do you think can interrupt your pain processing ability? If you've experienced anything like I have, there are moments where you just can't change the pain response to anything beyond pain. What normally feels really good is just not working. Other than a particularly mean sadist who loves to challenge pain processing and break your ability to process pain (KnyghtMare!), there are a number of things that can block your ability to positively process pain.

6: What Can Block Pain Management?

Let's think about the things that we need to actively process pain and make play enjoyable for both parties. You need focus, trust, little to no distraction, appropriate mood, and a healthy and rested body. Any of these things can fall out of balance and then you may have issues processing pain.

Mood

Mood is separated in two parts; your emotional state and the environmental mood set up by the scene.

If you are in a bad mood you won't respond to pain well. You may fight the pain or store it up without a release mechanism. A negative mindset can also make pain seem more intense and bring you to your limit a lot faster and with less positive benefits. Did you have a bad day at work and are still angry? What about your household chores; does seeing the dishes incomplete make you frustrated? You'll want to work on your mood before you play.

Bad moods aren't typically a good time to play for the Top either, so if you notice that your Top is in a bad mood it might be a good time to postpone and decide to play later on.

The mood that was established for the scene can also hinder your pain processing. If the music is unpleasant, the room is too warm or too cool or there's just too much clutter you may lose the ability to focus on the pain and use your processing techniques correctly. Mixing different play types can be distressing to you as well. Take for example, if your Top starts out with a lighthearted sensation scene and then it shifts to an intense pain scene your body may not be able to translate that change in the way you need to. In this case, working with the Top to learn better transitions in play would be a benefit for your management.

Focus

If you cannot focus you will not be able to control the way you manage the pain. Any kind of distractions can do it; from financial worries, incomplete tasks, family strife to the

6: What Can Block Pain Management?

simple paper cut bothering you can knock you off your game. Distractions at play parties are a common challenge with focus. I personally use blindfolds and ear plugs at play parties to help me maintain focus on what is going on with me and not on what is going on around me or what the couple nearby is talking about. Losing your focus on what's going on also inhibits your responses, so you are actually robbing your Top of their enjoyment. If you are unable to focus, take a break and perhaps play another time.

If you just focus on the pain without any pain management it will make it more intense. Some novice bottoms think that if they focus directly on the pain that they will get through the session faster and with guts of steel. Sure, if you make the pain more intense and don't try any of the management techniques talked about previously, you are going to have to end the scene faster because you will reach your edge long before your Top wants you to. Also, toughing it out and acting macho could get you hurt; and not in a good way. If you find yourself unable to do anything but grit your teeth through the pain it would be best if you stop play and try another time.

Fear/Anxiety

Fear and anxiety will make pain feel more intense. Intense pain will add to your fear and anxiety. It's a circle of distrust that can be temporary or permanent. There is no doubt that some of the activities we do can cause fear and anxiety, but if there's a foundation of trust with your partner this fear will be temporary. This is a positive form of fear.

If however, this fear and anxiety is a negative result of things and the trust is broken for other reasons, then the pain you experience will be so intense that it will drive your fear higher and could lead to panic.

Terror/Panic

Beyond fear is terror and beyond anxiety is panic. These are similar to fear and anxiety but to a much greater degree. When you experience these emotions it's practically impossible to be able to process pain in any way. Your mind

6: What Can Block Pain Management?

has superseded your pain processing with these other emotions. Terror and panic make it impossible to focus.

Most people can't safely maintain a state of terror or panic for very long. The body tends to shut down and exhaustion sets in. Bottoms experiencing panic are also likely to lash out at their Top, injure themselves by straining too hard or have emotional breakdowns.

Triggers

A trigger is a reminder of past trauma. It can be a stimulus such as a smell, sound, or sight that triggers feelings of the trauma. This reminder can cause a person to have overwhelming feelings of sadness, anxiety, or panic. It may also cause people to have flashbacks. A flashback is a vivid often negative memory that can appear without warning. It can cause someone to lose track of their surroundings and "relive" a traumatic event.

Triggers can take on many forms. Sometimes triggers are predictable. In other cases, triggers may surprise you. When people who may have experienced past trauma engage in

SM play, there is a possibility of a previously unknown trigger event. Communicating with your partner before play, to notify them of potential triggers can help prevent them but it isn't always the case. In some cases, a sensory trigger can cause an emotional reaction before a person realizes why they are upset.

Learn how to best take care of yourself during a trigger event by identifying what you need for self-care and aftercare. Talk with your partner about what you want them to do for you if they hit a trigger during play, for example, hugs and quiet time or no contact at all to allow you to process and recover from the event. Understanding how to help someone going through a panic attack could help you.

The next time you prepare for pain play of any sort, see where your mind is at. Are you prepared for the active processing you will need to do or is your focus on something that will only make the experience more difficult for you?

6: What Can Block Pain Management?

The Invisible Barrier of Your False Edge

The false edge. This is the limit we impose on ourselves as far as pain tolerance, but isn't where our actual pain tolerance lies. Together, we'll work on trying to break free of the false edge and soar into heightened pleasures with pain.

Passing The False Edge

Over the course of this book you've hopefully learned how the body processes pain, the benefits of pain processing in play, the negative things that can hinder our pain enjoyment and techniques to employ to be able to play longer and enjoy pain more.

What is the false edge?

When you are playing with pain and you reach a moment where you are thinking of nothing but wanting it to stop, but the pain you are feeling isn't why you are considering it – think. Is it fear that is keeping you from continuing? Perhaps uncertainty of what could come next; or how far you are willing to go? You may just have reached your false edge.

The false edge is not a physical limitation; that's a limit. The false edge is the sense you are going to lose control if you continue. There comes a moment in intense play where you can feel afraid if you allow your Top to continue. What's really happening is you fear letting go of the last bit of control that you have; the control over your reactions.

The goal of an intense pain scene, where masochists find the most joy is the ability to let go and get past the false edge. A person past the false edge will begin to start reacting instinctively rather than in a controlled method. This is a far more relaxed and freer feeling that one might realize.

6: What Can Block Pain Management?

Why go beyond the false edge?

If you can relax and let your body take over your pain processing, your reactions will be raw and genuine. Breaching your false edge allows you to play longer and harder.

Which in turn is a greater benefit for the masochist and the sadist.

You must go beyond your false edge to reach your true edge. Your true edge is that ultimate limit that you probably can't even fathom right now because you've only thought of your limit being pain bearing. But once you've learned how to manage pain better and process it efficiently you just might surprise yourself!

Find out how far you can really go.

7: Important Tips for Negotiating Pain Play

When you engage in pain play with someone you haven't played with before, or don't have the experience of pain play with, you have a bit more negotiation to do than what would be typical. Remember that negotiation does not have to be formal, just having a discussion before play so that you both are on the same page will be a huge help to making sure you both get what you want out of the scene.

With that said, there are a few important topics to cover when there will pain processing during play.

7: Important Tips for Negotiating Pain Play

Be More Specific About Pain – When a Tool is More Than Sting or Thud

When I first learned about BDSM, and then that I enjoyed pain play as a masochist, there was a moment when a Top that I had asked to play with asked me a very specific question, at least I thought it was specific at the time. "Stingy or thuddy?"

Did I prefer sting or thud when it came to the type of pain that I enjoyed? At the time, I heartily responded sting. But now that I've got a few years under my belt I realized that those two phrases are pretty vague and don't cover the wide variety of pain that you can experience in a scene depending on the type of tool used or the intensity of the tools. Sure, they cover a majority of the impact tools used, but that's not the only way to experience pain in play, is there?

Why did we get stuck on sting and thud as the only two possibilities to describe what we like in pain play anyway? I don't think we've expanded the types of play activities that much in recent years to not know of other sensations than stingy and thuddy to describe them. I mean, pain management in medical situations, there are more ways to describe what kind of pain you're feeling, why haven't we applied any of them?

- aching
- biting
- blunt
- burning
- cold
- comes and goes
- constant
- crushing
- cutting
- dragging
- dull
- excruciating
- frightful

7: Important Tips for Negotiating Pain Play

- gnawing
- hot
- intense
- nagging
- nauseating
- niggling
- numb
- penetrating
- piercing
- pins and needles
- pricking
- radiating
- scratchy
- sharp
- shooting
- smarting
- sore
- spreading
- stabbing
- stinging
- tender
- throbbing
- tingling

- tiring
- unbearable

Not all of these can describe the pain we experience when we play with a partner, but a lot of them could! I've got a different list. It's shorter and perhaps can help you really nail down what sort of pain you enjoy and which you'd like to avoid. So, let's break it down a bit and really cover more than sting and thud.

Types of Pain You Could See During a BDSM Scene:

Direct, Acute - This type of pain is a sharp, intense pain. Common tools that deliver direct pain are single tail whips, cats and lightweight floggers, as well as bare-handed spanking, paddles, tawses, and belts.

Surface - Surface pain is slappy and spread out. It covers a larger area and is most often skin deep. Tools that often deliver surface pain are floggers, paddles as well as bare-handed spanking and slapping. Abrasion is also a form of surface pain and comes from scratching and scraping tools and fingernails.

Deep Tissue - Deep tissue pain is just as you might think. This impacts the muscles and inner tissues. Methods to experience deep tissue pain are kicking, punching, wrestling, and some heavy floggers.

Sustained - Sustained pain is the pain that you have to endure. It's a pain that starts and then is maintained or slowly gets worse as your endurance is taxed. It is frequently present in suspension and rigorous bondage in the form of compression as well as things like clothespins and needles.

Joint or Muscle Pain - This is pain that is caused by fatigue or strain. Restricting bondage can cause joint and muscle pain. Suspension bondage can cause joint and muscle pain. Any time you pull your body into contortions where it's not at rest can cause this form of pain.

Electric - This is a unique pain that you can only get when doing electrical play. Things like Tens units and violet wands can bring out this pain.

Two-Stage Pain - This is the type of pain that has either a cycle or a reverberation. Clothespins could be considered 2-stage pain inducers because you have the initial pain when they are put on, then things dull until you take them off. But the big ones for me are canes and pressure points. Canes definitely have a direct component to them, but also when

7: Important Tips for Negotiating Pain Play

given at a higher intensity you have a pain that is direct and then a secondary sharp reverberation pain as your tissues responds to the compression.

Emotional - Emotional pain is probably one of the harder ones to pinpoint and certainly not one where any form of common pain processing that we've talked about. Emotional pain comes from fear and suffering, from feelings of degradation and humiliation.

Nerve Pain - Nerve pain is a burning, stabbing, tingling pain. It is my personal opinion that this pain is never good pain and should be addressed ASAP when you start to experience it. Nerves can be damaged very easily if the pain is ignored and often that damage is permanent.

Why We Need More Than "Sting" and "Thud"

Since I've listed a few more pain descriptors than sting and thud, I think you'll agree that we could definitely use a more specific list then just these two words. I'm going to use them more when I negotiate with others for pick up play. It will make things easier I think and we might just be on the same page a lot faster.

Thinking further about why we might want to describe something with more than sting and thud comes from personal perceptions of pain. I've been on the receiving end of a tool that the Top swore up and down was a thuddy tool, only to be shocked, surprised and a bit miffed when it turned out to bite, a sharp, stingy surface pain.

As we learn more about what sorts of pain we look for in a scene, and what sorts of pain processing we need to employ to process different pain, we'll have a better understanding

7: Important Tips for Negotiating Pain Play

of what will create a playtime that we will enjoy and crave. Starting with being able to define how a tool feels, and what sort of pain it delivers is a great first step for you to build a scene that will work for you and a partner.

Ultimately, we want to play with tools and toys that cause pain, that's what makes us a pain play enthusiast and some of us as masochists. So let's stop using just "sting" and "thud" and get into more specific terms when we play. We'll go further and it will build a working knowledge for how to process the sorts of pain you truly enjoy that much easier.

Describe How You Process Pain

Let the top know if you tend to laugh or cry, go silent or need space to move around. As you learned, we all have different ways to respond to pain; some good and some bad. Letting the person you are playing with know what to expect is helpful and beneficial not only for you, but for them.

Tops that are aware of positive pain processing can help a bottom who isn't doing well during a scene work towards better processing without disrupting the play – so knowing in advance how someone tends to respond to pain play is a good thing to know.

If you don't know how you respond to pain, tell them that also.

Discuss Your Pain Processing Goal

We learned in this guide that there are several goals that bottoms tend to reach for when playing with pain. From catharsis to pleasure, service or sub space; knowing what you want to reach for during a specific play scene can help the Top navigate towards that end.

7: Important Tips for Negotiating Pain Play

If Sub Space is to Be Avoided

When I want to move about in pain play and be an active participant I will tell my Dominant that I do not want to reach sub space. With this knowledge he will use tactics that pull me out of spacey feelings at regular intervals during play so that we can keep going.

Another reason to avoid sub space is if the partner you are playing with is new to you. In sub space your common sense and reasoning skills fail. It's also possible to be unable to safe word out of play and limits can be breached. If you feel that sub space is not a safe goal for the current play partner or scene experience then make sure to inform them that you want to avoid sub space.

Know how to avoid sub space. There are ways to keep a bottom from entering sub space. Things like a change in the level of pain, or the type of pain; thud vs. sting can keep a bottom from heading into subspace. Even changing tools or asking the bottom to communicate with you can bring them away from the brink. If you know that any of these things, or something else entirely will keep you from sub space, tell the Top of the scene so that they can comply with your wish to avoid sub space.

Discuss Aftercare

Never assume that aftercare is a given or that the same type of aftercare is desired. You may require a different type of aftercare from a pain play scene than you do when no pain is involved. Once you learn what that is, make sure you negotiate that with your Top. If the top you are playing with does not perform aftercare, find a surrogate. It is not the Top's job to provide aftercare unless negotiated first. So find the aftercare you need if they do not provide it.

In Closing

In the end your way to processing pain will be unique to you and hopefully will teach you that the pleasure you receive through pain, is also the pleasure that Top's receive from you. Take what you've learned in this book and apply it to your play. Bring your pain play deeper, more meaningful and intense.

About lunaKM

Luna Carruthers has been a submissive since 2004. She is married to her Dominant partner, KnyghtMare. She has been in leadership of several local BDSM communities and has presented on topics about D/s dynamics and BDSM. In 2009, she started SubmissiveGuide.com, a community and knowledge resource for submissives of all walks of life. She focuses on common sense advice and information to bring submission into reality for many.

About Submissive Guide

Submissive Guide is dedicated to helping submissives understand themselves and the service they wish to provide; from sexual to domestic, personal assistant to pain slut and everything in between.

Subguide prides itself on being the largest resource for submissives of all types, from novice to highly skilled. Since 2009, we've provided articles, ebooks, live chat, ecourses and more, all geared to helping submissives explore their personal journey in submission.

We invite you to come browse the extensive library of over 1500 articles or pick up a resource or two to add to your own collection.

https://submissiveguide.com

Other Books by Luna Carruthers

All existing and future publications by Luna Carruthers can be purchased through Amazon or through her website SubmissiveGuide.com.

Submissive Reflection: A Journey of Rediscovery and Affirmation is a perfect guide to helping you do that soul-searching and to really pinpoint where you are in your submissive journey right now. You'll gain understanding about how your personality, past relationships and inner code of ethics work together to define your submissive identity. Whether you have a partner or not, this workbook has the tools and knowledge to help you understand your place in submission.

Lessons in Submissive Speech: Learning the Art of Speaking Submissively will give you the tools you need to learn appropriate responses, how to address people and submissive speaking skills for a number of common situations. As a submissive, you may not know that there are a variety of approaches to the way you handle speaking to others. You need help from someone who has done it all before and can show you how to speak demurely and with a humble attitude.

The Online Submissive: Creating a Working Long-Distance or Online D/s Relationship Through Technology is a self-help book for submissivews who are exploring BDSM and power exchange relationships with the help of technology. You'll learn how long-distance and online D/s relationships develop and grow, and how to keep them thriving using today's technology and your own creativity.

Also Available as PDF Ebooks:

https://submissiveguide.com/store

Made in the USA
Monee, IL
16 April 2024

56765923R00066